Mariamne

Voltaire

Translation by William F. Fleming

Contents

Dramatis Personæ. 3

Act I. 4

Act II. 11

Act III. 18

Act IV. 27

Act V. 33

Dramatis Personæ

Varus, a Roman Prætor, Governor of Syria.
Herod, King of Palestine.
Mariamne, Wife of Herod.
Salome, Sister of Herod.
Albinus, Friend to Varus.
MAZAEL, Herod's Minister.
IDAMAS, Herod's Minister
Nabal, an old Officer under the Asmonæan Kings.
Eliza, Confidante of Mariamne.
Herod's Guard, Attendants on Varus, Herod, and Mariamne.

This piece was produced in 1724.

ACT I.

SCENE, Jerusalem.

SCENE I.

Salome, Mazael.

Mazael: It is enough: the power of Salome, By all acknowledged, and by all obeyed, On its firm basis stands immovable: I fled to Azor, with the lightning's speed, Even from Samaria's plain to Jordan's spring, And quick returned: my presence there indeed Was needful, to cut off the aspiring hopes Of Israel's moody race: thy brother Herod, So long detained at Rome, was almost grown A stranger in his kingdom; and the people, Ever capricious, turbulent, and bold, Still to their kings unjust, aloud proclaimed, That Herod was condemned to slavery By haughty Rome; and Mariamne, raised To the high rank of her proud ancestors, Would from the blood of our high-priests select A king, to rule o'er conquered Palestine. With grief I see, she is by all adored; Her name the dear delight of every tongue; Israel reveres the race from whence she sprang, Even to idolatry: her birth, her beauty, And, above all, her sorrows, melt the hearts Of the rude rabble, who, thou knowest, detest And rail at us. They call her their dear sovereign, And seem to threaten thee with swift destruction. I saw the fickle multitudes alarmed With idle tales like these, but soon I taught them Another lesson; soon I made them tremble: Told them great Herod, fraught with double power, And armed with vengeance, would ere long return: His name alone struck terror to their souls, They saw their folly then, and wept in silence.

Salome: Thou toldest them truth, for Herod comes, and soon Shall make rebellious Sion bend beneath him. Antony's favorite is Cæsar's friend; Fortune attends him, at his chariot wheels Submissive chained: his subtle policy Is equal to his courage, and he rises With added strength and glory from his fall: The senate crown him.

Mazael: But when Mariamne Shall see her husband, where will be thy power? That haughty rival o'er the king had ever A fatal influence that supplanted thee; And her proud spirit, still inflexible, And still revengeful, holds its enmity: Her safety must depend on thy destruction, And mutual injuries nourish mutual hate. Dost thou not dread her all-subduing charms, Those lordly tyrants o'er the vanquished Herod? For five years past, ever since their fatal marriage, Hath his strange passion for her still increased, By hatred fixed, and nourished by disdain. Oft have we seen the haughty monarch kneel Before her feet, her eyes indignant turned In fury from him, whilst in vain he sued For softer looks than she would deign to give. How have we seen him rage, and sigh, and weep, Abuse, and flatter, threaten and implore! Mean in his rage, and cruel in his love; Abroad a hero, and a slave at home: He punished an ungrateful barbarous race, And, reeking with the father's blood, adored The daughter; raised the dagger to her breast, Guided by thee, then dropped it at her feet. At Rome indeed, whilst from her sight removed, The chain was loosened; but 'twill re-unite When he returns, and shall again behold The fatal charms which he so long admired: Those powerful eyes are ever sure to please, And will resume their empire o'er his heart: Her foes will soon be humbled, and if she But gives the nod, must fall a sacrifice To her resentment. Let us guard against it, And court that power which we can never destroy: Respect well-feigned may win her to our purpose.

Salome: No: there are better methods to remove Our fears of Mariamne.

Mazael: Ha! what means?

Salome: Perhaps even now she dies.

Mazael: And wilt thou dare To do a deed so desperate? If the king—

Salome: The king assists me in the work of vengeance, And has consented: Zares is arrived At Solyma; my instrument of wrath Waits for his victim: know, the time, the place, The hand to execute, are ready all: To-day it must be done.

Mazael: Hast thou then gained At last the victory? Could the king believe thee? Spite of his passion, will he yield up all, And act as thou commandest?

Salome: Not so: my power Is more confined: scarce could I urge to vengeance, With all my arts, his long-reluctant soul, But I availed me of his absence from her: Whilst Herod lived, exposed to all her charms, Thou knowest I led a life of wretchedness, Of doubt and fear, uncertain of my fate; When, by a thousand crooked paths, at last I found a passage to his heart, and thought I had secured it, Mariamne came; And, when he saw her, all was lost again; My arts all baffled by a single glance: Yes, the proud queen was mistress of my life, And might have taken it: had she known the way To manage well her easy lover's fondness, Herod had signed the mandate for another, And not for Mariamne; then the blow I meant for her had fallen on Salome: But I have made her pride assist my vengeance, And I have only now to point the dart, Which her own hand hath fashioned, to destroy her. Thou mayest remember well the fatal time That blasted all our hopes; when, Antony Subdued. Augustus took the reins of empire, Each Eastern monarch trembled on his throne: Amongst the rest my hapless brother feared, With his protector, he had lost his crown. Resistance now was vain, and naught remained But to address the conqueror of the world In lowliest terms, and ask forgiveness of him. Call back that dreadful day, when Herod, driven Even to despair, beheld proud Mariamne Spurn at his offered love and kind farewell; Heard her with anguish heap reproaches on him; Call for a father's and a brother's blood, Shed by her tyrant husband: Herod flew To me, and told his griefs; I seized the moment Propitious to my vengeance, and regained A sister's power o'er his distressed heart; Inflamed his rage, and sharpened his despair; Dipped in fresh poison the envenomed dart That pierced his soul: then, desperate in his wrath, Thou heardest him swear to exterminate the race Of Hebrews, and destroy its poor remains; Condemn the mother, and cut off her sons From their inheritance: but soon to rage Succeeded love; one look from her disarmed His vengeance. I, with double eagerness, Pressed his departure, and at length prevailed: He left her; from that hour I was successful; My frequent letters kept up his resentment, And, absent from her, all his rage returned: He blushed in secret for his weakness past, And by degrees, as I removed the veil, His eyes were opened: Zares caught with me The favorable hour, and painted her In blackest colors; told him of her power, Her interest, friends, and the seditious faction, The partisans of the Asmonæan race. But I did more, I raised his jealousy; He trembled for his glory, and his life: Continual treasons had alarmed his soul, And left it ever open to suspicion: Whate'er he fears, still ready to believe, He is not able to distinguish guilt From innocence; in short, I fixed his soul, Guided his hand, and made him sign the mandate.

Mazael: 'Twas nobly done: but what will Varus say, The haughty prætor, will he see unmoved A deed so daring? he's thy master here, And, unconfirmed by Rome, thy power is nothing. From Varus' hand thy brother must receive His crown; nor can he act as sovereign here Till the proud prætor shall restore it to him. Will Varus, thinkest thou, e'er permit a queen, Left to his care, to fall a sacrifice? I know the Romans well, they ne'er forgive Such rude contempt of their authority. Thou wilt bring down the storm on Herod's head; Their thunder's always ready; those proud conquerors Are jealous of their rights, and take, thou knowest, Peculiar pleasure in the fall of kings.

Salome: Fear not for Herod, Cæsar is his friend, And Varus knows it, therefore will respect him: Perhaps this Roman means to manage all, But be it as it may, my aim is vengeance; I'm on the verge of glory or of shame; To-morrow, nay, to-day may change the scene: Who knows if e'er hereafter I shall find An hour propitious to me, who can tell If Herod will be steady to his purpose? I know his weakness, and I must prevent it, Nor give him time to say, it shall not be. When it is done, let Varus rage, and Rome Pour forth her threats, it shall not damp my joys: The Romans are not here my worst of foes; No, I have more to fear from Mariamne; I must subdue her rival powers, or perish: But Varus comes this way, we must avoid him: Zares ere now should have been here: I'll hence And meet him; fare thee well.—If there be need, My soldiers at the least alarm are ready, And will defend us.

SCENE II.

Varus, Albinus, Mazael, Attendants Onvarus.

Varus: Salome and Mazael— They seem to shun us; in their eyes I read Their terrors; guilt hath reason to be fearful, And dread my presence.—Mazael, stay: go, tell Thy cruel master his designs are known; His wicked instrument is now in chains, And should have met the death he merited, But my regard for Herod bids me hope That he will soon behold the snare they laid. Punish the traitors, and revenge the cause Of injured virtue: if thou lovest thy king, If thou regardest his honor or his peace, Calm his wild rage, embitter not his soul With vile suspicions, and remember, slave, Rome is the scourge of villainy; remember That Varus knows thee; that he's master here, And that his eyes are open to detect thee Away: let Mariamne be obeyed, And treated like a queen; observe her well, And, if thy life be dear to thee, respect her.

Mazael: My lord—

Varus: Begone: you know my last commands; Reply not, but obey them.

SCENE III.

Varus, Albinus.

Varus: Without thee, And thy well-timed advice, thou seest, my friend, The beautous Mariamne had been lost.

Albinus: Zares' return raised my suspicions of him; His most officious care to avoid thy presence, And troubled features, I must own, alarmed me.

Varus: How much I owe thee for the important service! By thee she lives; by thee my heart once more Shall taste its noble happiness, the best And fairest treasure of the virtuous mind, The happiness to succor the oppressed.

Albinus: Such generous cares befit the soul of Varus; Thy arm was ever stretched to help the wretched; Still hast thou born Rome's thunder through the world, And only conquered but to bless mankind; Would I might say thy pity dictates here, And not thy love!

Varus: Must love then be the cause? Who would not cherish innocence like hers? What heart, howe'er indifferent, would not plead So fair a cause? who would not die to save her?

Albinus: Thus the deceitful passion hides itself In virtue's garb, and steals into the heart: Thy hapless flame—

Varus: Albinus, I confess it; The wretched Varus dotes on Mariamne: Thou seest my naked heart, which fears not thee, Because thou art my friend: judge then, Albinus, How must her dangers have alarmed my soul! Her safety and her welfare are my own; Death in its ugliest form were welcome to me, If it could make my Mariamne happy.

Albinus: How altered is the noble heart of Varus! Love has avenged himself of all thy flights; No longer do I see the virtuous Roman, Severe and unimpassioned, 'midst the crowd Of rival beauties, who solicited His wandering eyes, regardless of their charms.

Varus: To virtue then, thou knowest, and her alone, I paid my vows: in vain corrupted Rome Offered her venal beauties to my eyes; Their pride disgusted, and their arts displeased; False in their vows, and in their vengeance cruel: I saw their shameless fronts all covered o'er With foul dishonor: vanity, ambition, Caprice, and folly, bore the name of love; Such conquests were unworthy of thy friend. At length the power I had so long contemned Indignant saw me from his Eastern throne, And soon subdued; it was my fate to rule O'er Syria's melancholy plains: when heaven Had to Augustus given the vanquished world, And Herod, midst a crowd of kneeling kings, Fell at his feet, and sued for his protection, Hither I came, and fatal to my peace Was Palestine, for there I first beheld her. The melancholy theme of every tongue Was Mariamne's woes; all wept her fate, Doomed to the arms of an inhuman husband, Who slew the father of his lovely bride: Thou knowest what miseries she had suffered since, Her sorrows only equalled by her virtue: Truth, ever banished from the courts of kings, Dwells on her lips, and all the art she knows Is but the generous care to serve the wretched. Her duty is her law; her innocence, Calm and serene, contemns the tyrant's power, And pardons her oppressor; even solicits My aid to save the man who would destroy her. Her virtues, her misfortunes, and her charms United, are too powerful for my soul; I love her, my Albinus; but my love Is not a passion which one day creates, And in another is forgotten; no: The heart she has subdued is not the slave Of loose desire, but by her virtue fired, Means to revenge but never to betray her.

Albinus: But if the king, my lord, has gained from Rome Permission to return.

Varus: Ay, that I fear: Alas! myself did move the senate for him. Perhaps already he returns to empire, And this abhorred mandate is his own; The first sad proof of his authority: It may be fatal to him. Varus' power May soon be lost, but O! his love remains; Yes, I will die in Mariamne's cause; The world shall weep her fate, and I avenge it.

ACT II.

SCENE I.

Salome, Mazael.

Salome: Thou seest we are ruined; Mariamne triumphs, And Salome's undone: that lingering Zares, How tedious was his voyage, as if the sea Unwillingly transported him! whilst Herod Flies with the winds to empire and to love: But sea and land, the elements, the heavens, All, all conspire with Varus, to destroy me. Ambition, thou hast plunged me deep in woe; Why did I listen to thy fatal voice? I knew his foolish heart would soon relent; Even now I fear he has revoked the mandate, And all the harvest of my toil is grief And danger, that still wait on high condition Stripped of its power: already fawning crowds Adore my rival, and insult my fall: My feeble glories, all eclipsed by her, Shall shine no more, for this new deity Must now be worshipped: but this is not all, My death, I know, must crown the triumph; she Can never reign whilst Salome survives; She will not spare a life so fatal to her. And yet, O shame, O infamous submission! My pride must stoop to vile dissimulation, To soothe her vanity with feigned respect, And give her joy of—Salome's destruction.

Mazael: Despair not, Madam, arms may yet be found To conquer this proud queen: I ever feared Her powerful charms, and Herod's weakness for her; But if I may depend on Zares, still In the king's bosom dwells determined hate, And he has sworn that she shall die: the blow Is but suspended till he comes himself To execute his vengeance; but, meantime, Whether his heart be sharpened by resentment, Or moved by love, it is enough his hand Once signed the mandate: Mariamne soon Will swell the tempest, and eternal discord Shall rankle in their hearts: I know them well: Soon will she light again the torch of hatred, Revive his doubts, and work her own destruction: With new disdain will irritate his soul: Rely upon herself, and mark her ruin.

Salome: O! 'tis uncertain; I can never wait Such tardy vengeance; I have surer means; Danger has taught me wisdom: this loud rage, These violent transports of the impassioned Varus, If I observe aright, can never flow From generosity alone, and pity Is seldom known by marks like these: the queen Has charms, and Varus may have charms for her. I know the power of Mariamne's beauty, Nor envy her the crowd of gazing fools, Who throw their flattering incense at her feet; The dangerous happiness may cost her dear: Whether she listens to the Roman's vows, Or with the conquest only means to soothe Her fickle pride, it is enough for me, If it preserves that power I must not lose O'er Herod's heart. Take care my faithful spies Perform their office; let them be rewarded, And sell me precious secrets.—Ha! she comes, Must I then see her?

SCENE II.

Mariamne, Eliza, Salome, Mazael, Nabal.

Salome: Joy to Mariamne: Herod returns, and Rome this day restores To me a brother, and to thee a husband. Thy cruel scorn had raised his just resentment, Which now subsides, and love has quenched the flame Which love alone inspired: his triumphs past, His future glories, all the senate's rights Reposed in him, the titles he has gained, All brought to lay at Mariamne's feet, Proclaim thy happiness: enjoy his heart; Enjoy his empire; I am pleased to see Thy virtues thus rewarded; Salome Shall lend her aid to join your hands together.

Mariamne: I neither looked for, nor desired your friendship: I know you, madam, and shall do you justice; I know by what mean arts, and treacherous falsehood, Your powerless malice has pursued my life. Perhaps thou thinkest my heart is like thy own, And therefore tremblest; but thou knowest me not: Fear nothing, for thy crimes and punishment Are both beneath my notice: I have seen Thy base designs, and have forgiven them: I leave thee to thy conscience, if a heart Guilty as thine is capable of feeling.

Salome: I've not deserved this bitterness and wrath From Mariamne: to my honest zeal, My conduct, and my brother, I appeal From thy suspicions.

Mariamne: I've already told thee, All is forgotten, I am satisfied, And I can pardon, though I can't believe thee.

Mazael: Now, by the power supreme, my royal mistress, Scarce could my pains—

Mariamne: Stop, Mazael, excuse Is added injury; obey the king, That is thy duty: sold to my oppressors, Thou art their instrument; perform thy office, I shall not stoop to make complaints of thee. Thou, Salome, mayest hence, and tell the king [To Salome.] The secrets of my soul; inflame his heart Once more with rage; I shall not strive to calm it: Instruct your creatures to deal forth their slander, I've left their vile attempts unpunished still; Content to use no arms against my foes, But blameless virtue, and a just disdain.

Mazael: What haughtiness!

Salome: 'Twill meet with its reward: It is the pride of art to punish folly.

SCENE III.

Mariamne, Eliza, Nabal.

Eliza: Why, my loved mistress, would you thus provoke A foe who burns with ardor to destroy you? Perhaps the rage of Herod is suspended But for a time, and yet may burst upon you. Death was departing, and thou callest him back, When thou shouldst strive to turn his dart aside: Thou hast no friend to guard or to defend thee; Varus, thy kind protector, must obey The senate's orders, and to distant realms Convey its high commands: at his request, And by thy kind assistance, Herod gained His power, and now the tyrant will return With double terror: thou hast furnished him With arms against thyself, and must depend On this proud master, to be dreaded more Because he loves, because his passion soured By thy disdain—

Mariamne: My dear Eliza, fly, Bring Varus hither: thou art in the right; I see it all; but I have other cares; My soul is filled with more important business: Let Varus come: Nabal, stay thou with me.

SCENE IV.

Mariamne, Nabal.

Mariamne: Thy virtues, thy experience, and thy zeal For Mariamne's welfare, have long since Deserved my confidence: thou knowest my heart, And all its purposes; the woes I feel, And those I fear: thou sawest my wretched mother,

Driven to despair, with tears imploring me To share her flight: her mind, replete with terror, Sees every moment the impetuous Herod, Yet reeking with the blood of half her race, Assassinate her dearest Mariamne. Still she entreats me, with my helpless children, To fly his wrath, and leave this hated clime; The Roman vessels might transport us soon From Syria's borders to the Italian shore; From Varus I might hope some kind protection, And from Augustus; fortune points the way For my escape, the only path of safety: And yet, from virtue or from weakness, which I know not, but my foolish heart recoils At flying from a husband's arms, and keeps, Spite of myself, my lingering footsteps here.

Nabal: Thy fears are groundless; yet I must admire them, Because they flow from virtue: thy brave heart, That fears not death, yet trembles at the thought Even of imaginary guilt: but cease Your causeless doubts; consider where you are; Open your eyes, and mark this fatal palace, Wet with a father's and a brother's blood. In vain the king denies the horrid deed; Cæsar in vain absolves him from the crime, Whilst the whole East pronounce him guilty of it. Think of thy mother's fears, thy injured sons, Thy murdered father, the king's cruelty, Thy sister's hatred, and what scarce my tongue Can mention without horror, though thy virtue Regardless smiles, thy death this day determined. If, undismayed by such a scene of woe, Thou art resolved to meet and brave thy fate, O still remember, still defend thy children: The king hath taken away their hopes of empire, And well thou knowest what dreadful oracles Long since alarmed thy fears, when heaven foretold, That a strange hand should one day join thy sons To their unhappy father. A wild Arab, Implacable and pitiless, already Hath half fulfilled the terrible prediction: After a deed so horrid, may he not Accomplish all the rest? From Herod's rage Nothing is sacred; who can tell but now, Even now he comes to act his bloody purpose, And blot out all our Asmonæan race? 'Tis time to guard against him, to prevent His guilt, and stop his murderous hand; to save Those tender victims from a tyrant's sword, And hide them from the sight of such examples. Within thy palace from my earliest years Brought up, and by thy ancestors beloved, Thou seest me ready to partake thy fortunes Where'er thou goest: away then; break thy chains; Fly to the justice of a Roman senate; Implore them to adopt thy injured sons, And shelter their distress: such innocence And virtue will astonish great Augustus. If just and happy is his reign, as fame Reports, and conquered worlds in rapture bend The knee before him, if he merits all The honors he has gained, he must protect thee.

Mariamne: My doubts are vanished, and I yield to thee; To thy advice, and to a mother's tears; To my son's danger, to my own hard fate; Which dooms me yet perhaps to greater ills Than I have suffered. Go thou to my mother; When night shall throw her sable mantle o'er This seat of guilt, let some one give me notice That all is ready; since it must be done, I am prepared.

SCENE V.

Mariamne, Varus, Eliza.

Varus: I come, great queen, to know Your last commands; which, as the law of heaven. Shall be revered: say, must this arm avenge thee? Speak, and 'tis done: command, and I obey.

Mariamne: Varus, I'm much indebted to thy goodness, And, but my sorrows plead their own excuse, Should not be thus importunate; I know Thou lovest to help the wretched, therefore ask Thy generous aid: whilst Herod's doubtful fate Hung in the balance, and he knew not which Awaited him, a prison or a throne, I did solicit Varus in his favor; Spite of his cruelties, against my peace, Against my interest, I performed my duty. Now Mariamne for herself implores Thy kind protection; begs thee to preserve From most inhuman laws, her hapless sons, The poor remains of Syria's royal race. Long since I should have left these guilty walls, And asked the senate for some safe retreat; But whilst the sword of war filled half the world With blood and slaughter, 'twas in vain to seek For refuge in the scene of wild destruction: Augustus now hath given the nations peace, And spread his bounties o'er the face of nature: After the toils of hateful war, resolved To make the world, which he had conquered, happy: He sits supreme o'er tributary kings, And takes the poor and injured to his care: Who has so fair a title to his justice, As my unhappy, my defenceless children? Brought by their weeping mother from afar To ask his succor; he will shelter them, His generous hand will wipe off all our tears. I shall not ask him to revenge my cause, Or punish my proud foes; it is enough If my loved children, formed by his example, And by his justice taught, true Romans soon, Shall learn to rule of those who rule mankind. A mother's comfort, and her children's safety, Depend on thee: my woes will vanish all If thou wilt hear me; and thy noble heart Hath ever been the friend of injured virtue: To thee I owe my life: assist me now, Remove me, Varus, from this fatal palace; Grant my benighted steps a friendly guide To Sidon's ports, where now thy vessels lie. Not answer me! what means that look of sorrow? Why art thou silent? O! too well I see Thou wilt not hear the voice of wretchedness.

Varus: It is not so: I hear, and will obey thee: My guards shall follow thee to Rome: dispose Of them, of me; my heart, my life is thine. Flee from the tyrant, break the fatal tie; 'Tis punishment enough to be forsaken By Mariamne: never shall he behold thee; Thanks to his own injustice; and I feel Too well there cannot be a fate more cruel. Forgive me, but the thought of losing thee Hath drawn the fatal secret from my breast; I own my crime: but, spite of all my weakness, Know, my respect is equal to my love: Varus but wishes to protect thy virtue, But to avenge thy injuries, and die.

Mariamne: I hoped the great preserver of my life Would prove the guardian of my honor too; And to his pity only thought I owed His kind assistance; ne'er did I expect That he, of all men, should increase my sorrows; Or that, to crown the woes of Mariamne, I should be forced to tremble at thy goodness, And blush for every favor I received: Yet, think not, Varus, that thy passion, thus Declared, shall rob thee of my gratitude: My constant friendship shall be ever thine; I will forget thy love, but not thy virtues: Thou hadst my praise and my esteem till now, But longer converse may deprive thee of it; For thy sake therefore, Varus, I must leave thee.

SCENE VI.

Varus, Albinus.

Albinus: I fear you're troubled, sir; your color changes.

Varus: Albinus, I must own, my spirits droop; Pity, my friend, the weakness of a heart That never loved before: alas! I knew not How strong my fetters were, but now I feel, Nor can I break them: with what sweet demeanor, And lovely softness, did she chide my passion; Calm and unruffled, how her tranquil prudence Taught me my duty, and enforced her own; How I adored her even when she repulsed me! I've lost all hope, yet love her more than ever: Gods! for what dreadful trial of my faith Am I reserved?

Albinus: Wilt thou then aid her flight?

Varus: 'Tis a sad office.

Albinus: Art thou pleased so well With her disdain, as thus to make thyself Unhappy, and promote thy own destruction? What dost thou purpose?

Varus: Can I e'er forsake her? Can I rebel against her laws? my heart Were then unworthy of her. Hence my doubts. 'Twas Mariamne spoke, and I obey: Quick, let her leave the tyrant; let her seek Augustus; she has cause to fly, and Varus Has none to murmur or complain; at least She leaves me the sweet pleasure to reflect, That I have lived and acted but for her; Have broke her chains, have saved her precious life: Nay more: for I will sacrifice my love, Fly from those dangerous charms that would betray me, And imitate the virtue I adore.

ACT III.

SCENE I.

Varus, Nabal, Albinus,attendants Onvarus.

Nabal: The king, my lord, the happy Herod, comes Triumphant, and the Hebrews flock in crowds To meet him: Salome, alarmed and fearful Of her declining interest, joins his train Of fawning courtiers, soothes his pride, and strives By every art to gain him to her purpose; The priests attend, and strew their palms before him. With Herod comes the faithful Idamas, Deputed by his sovereign to attend The noble Varus; he will soon be here. Still hath he proved himself the constant friend Of Mariamne, and by wholesome counsels Softened the rage of his impetuous master: The queen, still wavering and irresolute, Condemns herself; her rigid virtue fears To do what danger tells her must be done: She quits the palace, then returns; meanwhile Her anxious mother, falling at her feet, Bathes them in tears, points to her weeping children, And trembling begs her to depart: she stops, And doubts, and much I fear will stay too long: 'Tis thou must hasten her; on thee alone Depends the safety of the noblest being Heaven e'er gave birth to. O preserve her; save The race august sprung from a line of kings; Save Mariamne. Are your guards all ready? May I inform her of it?

Varus: All's prepared: I gave them orders: she may go this moment.

Nabal: And wilt thou too permit a faithful servant To follow his loved mistress?

Varus: Go with her, Wait on her steps, and guard her as thy life: This hateful place deserves her not: may heaven, In pity to her sorrows, smile upon her; Light up a fairer sun to gild her journey, And bid the waves in smoother currents flow, Obedient to the sacred charge they bear! Thou, good old man, mayest follow and attend her; Thou art too happy, but thou hast deserved it.

SCENE II.

Varus, Albinus, Attendants Onvarus.

Varus: Already Herod comes; the trumpet's sound Speaks his return; unwelcome sound to me! I dread his presence: cruel as he is, Instant his wrath may fall on Mariamne: Would she had left forever these sad seats Of guilt and horror! would I might partake Her flight! but O! the more I love, the more I must avoid her: 'twere in me a crime To follow her; and all that Varus can— But Idamas approaches.

SCENE III.

Varus, Idamas, Albinus, Attendants Onvarus.

Idamas: Ere the king, My royal master, comes, with gratitude To pay thy bounties, and receive from thee The holy sceptre, say, wilt thou permit me?—

Varus: No more: your king may spare this idle homage, These practised arts of visionary friendship Amongst the great, drawn forth with pompous splendor But to amuse the gaping multitude And foreign to the heart: but say, at length Rome has consented; Herod is your king; Doth he deserve to reign? Is the queen safe, And will he spare the blood of innocence.

Idamas: May the just gods, who hate the perjured man, Open his eyes, now blinded by imposture! But who shall dive into his secret thoughts, Or trace the emotions of his troubled soul? Naught can we draw from him but sullen silence; Or if perchance the name of Mariamne Escape his lips, he sighs, and raves: this moment Gives secret orders, and the next revokes them: Herod detests the race from whence she sprang, And hates her more because he loved too well. Perfidious Zares, by thy order stopped, And by thy order freed, the artificer Of calumny and fraud, will serve the cause Of subtle Salome, whilst Mazael lends His secret aid: the jealous Herod listens To their suggestions; they besiege him closely; And their officious hatred still keeps truth At distance from him: this great conqueror, Who made so many potent monarchs tremble, This king, whose noble deeds even Rome admired, Whose name yet fills all Asia with alarms, In his own house beholds his glories fade: Torn by suspicions, and o'erwhelmed with grief; Led by his sister, hated by his wife: I pity him, and fear for Mariamne. Say, wilt thou not protect her?

Varus: 'Tis enough: Albinus, follow me, the queen's in danger: Away, for I must save the innocent.

Idamas: Will you not wait then for the king?

Varus: I know I should receive him here: it is my duty, For so the senate wills: but other cares Inspire me now, and other interests guide: 'Tis my first duty to protect the wretched. [Exit Varus.]

Idamas: What storms do I foresee? what new distresses Will soon o'ertake us? Now, O Israel's God, Change Herod's heart!

SCENE IV.

Herod, Mazael, Idamas,attendants OnHerod: **Herod**: Varus avoid me too! What horrors meet me here on every side! Good heaven! can Herod inspire naught but hatred And terror to mankind? Is every heart Thus shut against me? To myself disgustful, My people, and my queen; with grief oppressed I re-ascend my throne, and only come To see the sorrows my own hand hath made. O heaven!

Mazael: Be calm, my lord, let me entreat you.

Herod: Wretch that I am, what have I done!

Mazael: Ha! weeping! Shall Herod weep, the great, the illustrious king, The dread of Parthia, and the friend of Rome, For wisdom and for valor long renowned! O! think my lord, of those distinguished honors Which Antony and victory bestowed; Think of thy fame, when seen by great Augustus, He chose thee from a crowd of conquered kings, And marked thee for his friend: call back the time, When great Jerusalem, by thee subdued, Submitted to thy laws: by thee defended, Once more she shines with all her ancient lustre, And sees her sovereign crowned with fair success: Never was king in peace or war more happy.

Herod: There is no happiness on earth for me; Fate points its poisoned arrows at my breast; And, to complete my woes, I have deserved them.

Idamas: Permit me, sir, the freedom to observe, Your throne, by fears and jealousies surrounded, Would stand more firmly on love's nobler basis: The king who makes his people's happiness Secures his own; thy soul, thus racked with tortures, Might trace the poisoned waters to their spring. O, my lord, suffer not malicious tongues To wound the peace and honor of thy life; Nor servile flatterers to estrange the hearts Of those who long to serve their royal master: Israel shall then enamored with thy virtues—

Herod: And thinkest thou Herod might again be loved?

Mazael: Zares, my lord, still faithful to his charge, Burns with the same unwearied zeal to serve thee: He comes from Salome, and begs admittance.

Herod: What! both forever persecute me! No! Let not that monster e'er appear before me; I've heard too much already: hence, begone, And leave me to myself: what shall I do To calm my troubled soul? Stay, Idamas, And, Mazael, stay.

SCENE V.

Herod, Mazael, Idamas.

Herod: Behold this dreadful monarch, This mighty king, who made the nations tremble; Who knew so well to conquer and to reign. To break his chains, and make the world admire His wisdom and his power: behold him now, Alas! how little like his former self!

Mazael: All own thy greatness, and adore thy virtues.

Idamas: One heart alone resists, and that perhaps May still be thine.

Herod: No: Herod's a barbarian, Unworthy of his throne.

Idamas: Thy grief is just, And if for Mariamne—

Herod: Fatal name! 'Tis that condemns me; that reproaches still My tortured soul with cruelty and weakness.

Mazael: My lord, your goodness but augments her hatred; She loathes your sight, and flies from your embraces.

Herod: I courted hers.

Mazael: Indeed, my lord?

Herod: I did: This sudden change, this grief that hangs upon me, These shameful tears, do they not all declare That Herod is returned from Mariamne? With love and hatred mingled in my soul, I left the crowd of flatterers in my court, And flew to her: but what was my reward? How did we meet! in anger, frowns, and strife: In her indignant eyes I read my fate, And my injustice: she scarce deigned to cast A look upon me; even my tears availed not; They only served to make her scorn me more.

Mazael: You see, my lord, her soul's implacable, And never will be softened by indulgence; It but inflames her pride.

Herod: I know she hates me; But I've deserved it, and I must forgive her: She has but too much cause from one so guilty.

Mazael: Guilty, my lord? hast thou forgot her flights, Contempt, and pride, and wrath, and fierce resentment; Her father's plot, her own designs against thee, And all her race thy mortal foes? Hircanus Had oft betrayed thee; the Asmonæan league Was firmly knit; and by such dangerous powers, That nothing but a master-stroke could save—

Herod: No matter: that Hircanus was her father, I should have spared him; but I only listened To proud ambition, and the love of empire: My cruel policy destroyed her race; I killed the father, and proscribed his daughter: I wanted but to hate and to oppress, And heaven, to punish me, hath made me love her.

Idamas: To feel a passion for a worthy object Is not a weakness in us, but a virtue, Worthy of every good which heaven hath given thee; Esteem thy love amongst its choicest blessings.

Herod: What hath my rashness done! ye sacred manes, Hircanus, Oh!

Mazael: Banish the sad remembrance, And grant, kind heaven, the queen too may forget it!

Herod: Unhappy father! more unhappy husband! The injuries I have done my Mariamne Make her more dear: O! if her heart—her faith— But I have stayed too long: now, Idamas, I'll make amends for all; go, haste, and tell her, My soul, obedient to her will, shall lay My throne, my life, my glory at her feet: Amongst her sons I'll choose a successor. She has accused my sister as the cause Of her misfortunes, henceforth I disclaim her; A nearer tie demands the sacrifice, And Salome must yield to Mariamne: My queen shall rule with power unlimited!

Mazael: My lord, you will not—

Herod: Yes: I am resolved: I know her now; she is the choicest gift Of bounteous heaven; as such I shall revere her: What cannot love, the mighty conqueror, do? To Mariamne I shall owe my virtue. In savage pomp, and barbarous majesty, Too long hath Asia seen her sovereign rule Respected by his people; feared, admired, Yet hated still; with crowds of worshippers, But not one friend. My sister, whom long time This foolish heart believed, hath ne'er consulted My happiness, my interest, or my fame: For Salome, more cruel than myself, And more revengeful, dipped her hands in blood, And ruled my subjects with a rod of iron: Whilst Mariamne felt for the unhappy, Forgot her own distress to pity theirs, And told me all their sorrows: but 'tis past: Henceforth I will be just, but not severe; I'll strive to please her by promoting still The public weal: Judah shall bless my reign, For I am changed. From this auspicious hour, Far from my throne, shall every jealous fear Be now removed: I will dry up the tears Of the oppressed, and reign o'er Palestine, Not as a tyrant, but a citizen; Gain every heart to merit Mariamne's. O seek her, tell her how my soul repents; That my remorse is equal to my rashness. Run, fly, begone, and instantly return. What do I see? my sister? hence: O heaven, Finish the woes of my unhappy life!

SCENE VI.

Herod, Salome.

Salome: Well, sir, you've seen your dear deceitful foe, And suffered more affronts; I know you have.

Herod: Madam, permit me to inform you, this Is not a time to add to my misfortunes; I would remove them: my imperious temper Made me more feared indeed, but more unhappy: Too long already o'er this house of sorrow Hath vengeance poured her black and deadly poison: The queen and you, thus at perpetual variance, Would be a spring of endless misery; therefore, My sister, for our mutual happiness, For thy repose and mine, 'tis best to part; Immediately, away: it must be so.

Salome: What do I hear! O fatal enemy!

Herod: A king commands, a brother begs it of thee: O may he ne'er again be forced to give One cruel order, ne'er take vengeance more, Nourish suspicions, or shed guiltless blood! Thou shalt no longer make my life a burden; Complain of me, lament thyself, but go.

Salome: Alas! my lord, I shall make no complaints; Since I am doomed to banishment by thee, It must be just, and fitting that I should be; For I have ever learned to make thy will My law: if thou commandest, I must obey; I never shall resent the injury, Or call on nature and the ties of blood, Or to attest, or vindicate my wrongs; The voice of nature's seldom heard by kings, The ties of blood are much too weak to bind them: I will not boast that tender friendship now Whose zeal offends thee; much less would I call To thy remembrance all my service past; One look I see from Mariamne soon Effaces all: but canst thou ever think She will forget the attempt upon her life Which Herod made? thee she must fear: thou therefore Shouldst dread her more: thou knowest her vows, her thoughts Are bent against thee, and whose counsels now Shall stay her vengeance? Where's the faithful heart Devoted to thee? where's the watchful eye, Ever awake, to guard the life of Herod? Who shall unravel all her subtle plots, Or who restrain her wrath? Dost thou believe, When thou hast put thy life within her power, That love will plead for thee? O no! such hate, Such scorn as hers, such desperate resentment—

Herod: Permit me, Salome, at least to doubt, At least delude me with the flattering hopes I may regain her heart: in this alone I wish to be deceived: show some regard, Some kind compassion for a brother's weakness: I must believe, thou knowest I've too much reason. Thy hatred was a barrier to our love: Thy malice hardened Mariamne's heart, And, but for thee, I had been less detested.

Salome: Couldst thou but know, O! couldst thou but conceive To what excess—

Herod: Sister, I'll hear no more: Let Mariamne threaten; let her take This loathesome life, for I am weary of it; So shall I perish by the hand I love.

Salome: It would be cruel to deceive you longer By guilty silence, or conceal her crimes: I know the dangerous hazard that I run By serving you; but I must speak, though death Were my reward: poor, blind, deluded husband, Enslaved by love for a vile worthless woman; Know Mariamne now, and know thy shame: 'Tis not her pride, her hatred, and disdain, Should make thee loathe her, but that—she is false; She loves another.

Herod: Mariamne love Another! barbarous sister! to suspect Her spotless virtue! Is it thus thou meanest To murder Herod? Are these poisoned darts The best farewell that thou canst leave thy brother? To light up discord, shame, and rage, and horror, In my distracted mind! Could Mariamne— But thou already hast too oft deceived me; Too long have I given credit to thy falsehood: Now heaven has punished my credulity, But it has ever been my fate to love Those who abhor me. You are all my foes; All sworn to persecute the wretched Herod.

Salome: Far from thy sight then—

Herod: Stir not hence, I charge thee; Another is beloved? Speak, tell me, who Must fall a sacrifice to Herod's vengeance? Pursue thy work, and make my woes complete.

Salome: Since I must speak—

Herod: Strike here: behold my heart: Who has dishonored me? Whoe'er he be, Thou, Salome, perhaps mayest answer for it, For thou art guilty: thou hast undeceived me: Now at thy peril speak.

Salome: No matter.

Herod: Well—

Salome: 'Tis—

SCENE VII.

Herod, Salome, Mazael.

Mazael: Bear not this indignity, my lord, The queen is fled, accompanied by Varus.

Herod: Varus, and Mariamne! gods! where am I?

Mazael: Varus, my lord, and all his troops have left The palace, and a secret band is placed About the walls to favor her retreat; Your Mariamne will be lost forever.

Herod: The charm is broke, and day shines full upon me: Come, Salome, acknowledge now thy brother, And know him by his wrath; let us surprise The infidel: now judge if Herod still Acts like himself, and like himself revenges.

ACT IV.

SCENE I.

Salome, Mazael.

Mazael: Never did fair appearance gild so well The specious covering of a happy falsehood: With what dexterity I played on him, And blended truth with artifice! But why Art thou dejected? art thou not restored To Herod's favor? Mariamne lost, Beyond recovery lost? Thou art avenged; The king's distracted. I am shocked myself When I behold the work of my own hands: Thou too hast seen the horrid spectacle, The trembling slaves all butchered by his hand. The queen half-dead, and fainting by their side, And Herod's arm uplifted as in act To murder her: the children bathed in tears Fall at his feet, and offer their own lives To save their mother's: canst thou wish for more, Or hast thou aught to fear?

Salome: I fear the king, I fear those fatal charms which he adores; That arm which oft uplifted falls as oft Inactive down; that anger which soon kindled Is soon extinct; which, doubtful still and blind, Exhausts its feeble powers in sudden transports: My triumphs, Mazael, are uncertain still; Twice has my fate been changed this day, and twice To hatred love succeeded: if he sees The queen again, we are undone.

SCENE II.

Herod, Salome, Mazael, Guards.

Mazael: He comes, And seems disturbed: what horror in his aspect!

Salome: Say, Herod, hast thou taken ample vengeance?

Mazael: I hope my royal master will forgive His faithful servant, who thus dares to speak Touching the queen: but Varus is her safeguard; Prevent his dark designs, and save thyself: The haughty prætor, resolute and bold, Will make a merit of destroying thee.

Herod: Alas! my sister, how have I been treated! Deceived, betrayed! help me to rail, to curse This dear ungrateful woman: now my heart Rests all its hopes on thy assisting friendship: Thou, Salome, wert made a sacrifice To my unhappy love for Mariamne; I numbered thee amongst my worst of foes; For her unkindness did I punish thee; But thou hast seen my tenderness betrayed, And, ere this day is past, we'll be revenged: Yes, she shall suffer for her fatal power O'er Herod's heart, that sighed for her alone. O how have I adored, and how detested, The faithless Mariamne! and thou, Varus, Shalt feel my wrath; thou art a Roman, therefore Thy life is safe; but I can punish thee In blood more precious, and a dearer self: Thou shalt behold the object of thy love, Who has preferred thee to her hated lord, Thou shalt behold her soon expire in torment Before thy eyes: dost thou not think Augustus Will praise my just severity?

Salome: No doubt He will, my lord, and would himself advise it. On the same altar where his friends adore him, He sheds the blood of foes: he teaches kings To rule and to be feared; let Herod mark And follow his example; thus alone Thy life can be secure: the queen must stand Condemned by all, and thou be justified.

Mazael: But make good use of this important moment, Whilst Varus is yet absent, and his forces Far from our walls; now seize her, and complete Thy easy vengeance.

Salome: Above all conceal From Israel's sons thy purpose and thy grief, And spare thyself the horror of a sight So dreadful; fly from this unhappy place, The witness of thy shame, that must recall A thousand mournful images; O hide From every eye thy sorrows and thy tears.

Herod: No: I must see her; face to face confound her; Force her to answer; hear her poor excuses: I'll make her tremble at the approach of death, And ask that pardon she shall never obtain.

Salome: My lord, you will not see her?

Herod: Fear me not; Her doom is fixed: vainly she hopes that love Will plead her cause; my heart is shut against her: Those eyes, which once were dangerous to my peace, Are harmless now; her presence will but raise My anger, not my love. Guards, bring her hither; I'll only see, and hear, and punish her. Sister, I would be private for a moment: [To the attendants.] Send Mariamne here: you may retire. [To the guards.]

SCENE III.

Herod: [Alone.] Art thou resolved to see her then? O Herod, Canst thou depend on thy own treacherous heart? Is not her guilt too plain, and have I not Been basely injured? Why then seek for more? What profit can this interview afford me? I know her thoughts already, know she hates me; Why lives she yet? revenge, thou art too slow! Unworthy Herod, coward as thou art, Go, see her, pardon, sigh again, and court Your haughty tyrant. No: to-night she dies: I've sworn it; the Asmonæan blood shall flow; I hate the race, and am abhorred by them. But see, she comes; heaven! what a mournful sight!

SCENE IV.

Mariamne, Herod, Eliza, Guards.

Eliza: Rouse up your spirits, madam, 'tis the king.

Mariamne: Where am I; whither do you lead me? O 'Tis death to look upon him.

Herod: How my soul Shudders at sight of her!

Mariamne: Eliza, help, Support me, I grow faint.

Eliza: This way.

Mariamne: What torment.

Herod: What shall I say to her? O heaven!

Mariamne: Well, sir, Your pleasure: wherefore am I ordered here? Is it to yield thee up the poor remains Of hated life, destructive to us both? Take it; strike here; I'll thank thee for the blow; The only gift I would accept from thee.

Herod: Then thou shalt have it: but first speak, defend, If possible, thy shameful flight, and tell me wherefore, When Herod's heart to thee alone indulgent, So oft offended, yet as oft forgave thee, The partner of my empire and my glory, What couldst thou purpose by so black a crime?

Mariamne: Is that a question fit for thee to ask? But 'tis not now a time for vain reproaches; Yet sure, my lord, if wretched Mariamne, Far from these walls had sought some kind retreat, If she for once had dared to violate A husband's rights, and swerve from her obedience, Think of my royal ancestors; remember My sufferings past, my present danger; think On these, my lord, and blame me if thou darest.

Herod: But when thy guilty passion for a traitor, For Varus—

Mariamne: Stop thy bold licentious tongue: My life is thine: but do not cover me With foul dishonor; let me pass at least Without a blush unspotted to the grave: Do not forget the sacred tie that bound us, That joined my honor and my fame with thine, As such I have preserved them: look on me; Strike here; thou art welcome: but remember still I am thy wife; pay some respect to me, And to thyself.

Herod: O! it becomes thee well To talk of sacred ties which thou hast broken: Perfidious woman! would not the proud scorn And hatred thou hast shown alone condemn thee?

Mariamne: Since thou already hast decreed my fate, What would avail my hatred or my love? What right hast thou to Mariamne's heart, Which thou hast filled with sorrow, and despair, And anguish: thou who, for these five years past, Hast marked my days with bitterness and woe; Thou fell destroyer of my guiltless parents. Where is my murdered father? cruel Herod! O! if thy rage had sought no blood but mine, Heaven be my witness, I had loved thee still, And blessed thee in my latest hour: but O! Do not pursue me, Herod, after death; Do not extend my woes beyond the grave, Preserve my children; do not punish them, Because they are mine, but act a father's part: Perhaps hereafter thou wilt know their mother; Perhaps shalt one day pity, when too late, The heart, which, never but by thee suspected, Could not disguise its griefs; the heart which still Preserved its virtue, and, but for thyself, Had loved thee, Herod.

Herod: Ha! what do I hear! What charm, what secret power controls my rage, And steals me from myself? O Mariamne!

Mariamne: O cruel Herod!

Herod: O my foolish heart!

Mariamne: For pity's sake behold my wretchedness, And take this hated life.

Herod: My own is thine, Forever thine; thou art my Mariamne: Banish thy fears; O thou wert sure to triumph When I beheld thee; make no more excuses, Thou art, thou must be innocent: I now Must tremble in my turn, and ask forgiveness: Wilt thou not pardon him who pardoned thee? Were our hearts made but to detest each other, To persecute ourselves? Let us at once End all our fears and all our pains together; Give me thy love, give me thy hand again.

Mariamne: Canst thou desire this hand? O heaven, thou knowest Herod's is stained with blood.

Herod: It is: I slew Thy father, and my king; but wherefore did it? To reign with thee: and what was my reward? Thy hatred; a reward I well deserved: I have no right to murmur or complain; Thy father's death, and the injustice done To thy unhappy children, are the least Of Herod's guilt; it reached even Mariamne, And for a moment I detested thee; Nay more, gave ear to foul suspicions of thee; 'Twill be the height of virtue to forgive me; The more my crimes, the more thy soul will show Its greatness: thou hast seen my weakness for thee, Take heed that thou abuse it not; for love And rage, thou knowest, by turns possess my soul; O give it ease; thou turnest aside thine eyes, Speak, Mariamne—

Mariamne: Such tumultuous transports Can never spring, I fear, from true repentance: Art thou sincere, and may I trust thee, Herod?

Herod: Thou mayest: what is there which thou canst not do If thou wilt cease to hate me? 'twas thy scorn That raised such furious tempests in my soul; It was the loss of Mariamne's heart That made me savage, barbarous, and inhuman: My tears shall wash away the mutual stain Of both our faults: and here I swear—

SCENE V.

Herod, Mariamne, Eliza, a Guard.

Guard: My lord, The people are in arms; they have destroyed The scaffold raised by Salome's command, And slain the officers of justice: Varus Assumes the sovereign power, he comes this way, And every moment we expect him here.

Herod: Ha! can it be! thus at the very instant When I was falling at thy feet, to raise Thy minion—

Mariamne: O my lord, can you believe—

Herod: Thou seekest my life, and thou shalt have it, traitress; But I will drag thee with me to the tomb, Spite of thyself, we there shall be united. A guard there, seize, and watch her.

SCENE VI.

Herod, Mariamne, Salome, Mazael, Eliza, Guards.

Salome: O, my brother, Venture not forth; for the rebellious Hebrews Are raised against you, and demand your life, Repeating still the name of Mariamne: They come even now to seize and take her from thee.

Herod: Away. I'll meet them unappalled: but thou Shalt answer for this insult: to thy care I leave her, Salome, guard well thy charge.

Mariamne: I fear not death, but call high heaven to witness—

Mazael: My lord, the Romans are already here.

Herod: And must I leave the guilty wretch unpunished? No: she shall bleed: it must be so: alas! In my sad state I can determine nothing; Death would be welcome; I'll away and meet it.

ACT V.

SCENE I.

Mariamne, Eliza, Guards.

Mariamne: Soldiers, retire, and leave your queen at least The mournful privilege to weep alone. [The guards retire to a corner of the stage.] Just heaven! is this at last my wretched fate? My noble blood, my title to a throne, All that could promise years of happiness, And days of pleasure, turned to deadly poison, Have filled my cup with bitterness and woe. O birth! O youth! and thou destructive beauty, Whose dangerous lustre but enflamed my pride, Flattering delusion! unsubstantial shade Of fancied bliss, O how hast thou deceived me! Beneath my fatal throne forever lurked Anguish and care, digging the grave that now Gapes to receive the dying Mariamne. In Jordan's flood I saw my brother perish, My father massacred by bloody Herod, Who now has doomed to death a guiltless wife: My virtue still remained, and that the tongue Of slander strives to wound: thou power supreme! Whose chastisements severe are but the proofs Of innocence, I ask not for thy aid, Nor for thy vengeance; my great ancestors Taught me to look on death unmerited Without a fear: take then my guiltless blood, But O! defend my fame: command the tyrant To spare my memory; let not clamorous falsehood Insult my ashes: virtue is avenged When she's respected. But what new alarm, What dreadful shrieks are these? the palace rings With loud confusion, and the din of arms: I am perhaps the cause, they fight for me: They force the doors: ha! what do I see?

SCENE II.

Mariamne, Varus, Eliza, Albinus, Soldiers.

Varus: Away: Hence ruffians; you who hold your queen in bondage, Vile Hebrews, hence:—you, Romans, do your office. [Herod's guards go off, chained by Varus's soldiers.] Now, Mariamne, thou art free; thou seest The tyrant could not bar my entrance here: Mazael lies bathed in his perfidious blood; At least my arm hath half avenged the cause Of injured majesty: haste, Mariamne, Seize the propitious moment, and secure A shelter from the storm: let us begone.

Mariamne: My lord, I cannot now accept thy bounty; After the vile reproach which Herod cast On my fair fame, I should indeed deserve it, Were I imprudent to receive the aid Thou profferest: I have much more cause to dread Thy kindness now than his barbarity; 'Twould be disgraceful thus to owe my life To Varus; honor says even this is guilt, And death alone can expiate my offence.

Varus: What wouldst thou do? alas! unhappy princess, A moment may destroy thee: the time presses; Still we're in arms, and Herod may succeed: Dost thou not fear his rage and his despair?

Mariamne: No: I fear naught but shame; and know my duty.

Varus: Am I then doomed forever to offend you? But I will do the work of vengeance for thee, Spite of thyself; once more I'll to the field; And, if the tyrant comes across me there, This arm—

Mariamne: Stop, Varus; I detest a triumph So dearly bought: know, sir, the life of Herod Demands my care: his rights—

Varus: Are forfeited By his ingratitude.

Mariamne: The sacred tie—

Varus: Is broken.

Mariamne: Duty hath united us.

Varus: But guilt divorces; therefore do not stay me, Revenge thyself, and save so many virtues.

Mariamne: Thou wouldst disgrace them.

Varus: He would take thy life.

Mariamne: Yet his is sacred still to Mariamne.

Varus: He killed thy father.

Mariamne: Varus, I know well What Herod did, and what I ought to do. Patient, I'll wait the fury of the storm, Nor by his crimes would justify my own.

Varus: O noble, brave, unconquerable heart! Ye gods, how many virtues have conspired To swell this tyrant's guilt! O Mariamne! The more thou shalt disclaim my proffered service, The more am I resolved to disobey thee. Thy honor disapproves what mine commands; But naught shall stop me, naught intimidate: I go to search the tyrant, and repair The hours I've lost in not avenging thee.

Mariamne: My lord—

SCENE III.

Mariamne, Eliza, Guards.

Mariamne: He's gone, and would not hear me: heaven! Let not more blood be shed; O spare my subjects; Pour all thy wrath on me, and spare even Herod!

SCENE IV.

Mariamne, Eliza, Nabal, Guards.

Mariamne: O Nabal, art thou here? what hast thou done With my dear children? where's my mother?

Nabal: Safe: The wrath of Herod reaches not to them: Thou art the only object of his fury, Which kindles at the hateful name of Varus: If he is conquered, Mariamne dies. The barbarous Zares is already sent With secret orders hither; thou mayest guess The purport, therefore now exert thy power: The people love thee; on their loyal zeal Thou mayest rely; the sight of thee will raise Their drooping hearts; let them behold thee: fly, My royal mistress, let us call the priests, All Judah's sons will rise to guard the race Of their loved kings: at length the hour is come, To conquer or to die: let me entreat thee—

Mariamne: True courage lies in knowing how to suffer, And not in stirring up rebellious crowds Against their sovereign: I should blush to think, That, anxious for itself, my fearful heart Had ever formed a wish for his destruction,

Or raised my hopes of safety on his death: No: heaven this moment has inspired my breast With rage less guilty, and a nobler purpose: Herod suspects me, he shall know me now; I'll rush into the battle; strive to part The king and Varus; cast myself before My husband's feet, and yield him up my life. I fled this morning from that dreadful vengeance Which now I search for: banished by his crimes, His danger has recalled me: honor bids, And I obey: I go to save his life Who thirsts for mine.

Nabal: Alas! to what extremes—

Mariamne: I'm lost: 'tis Herod.

SCENE V.

Herod, Mariamne, Eliza, Nabal, Idamas, Guards.

Herod: Did they see each other? Now, faithless wretch, thou diest.

Mariamne: Do not, my lord, 'Tis the last boon that I shall crave; O do not—

Herod: Begone—guards, follow her. [Guards carry off Mariamne.]

Nabal: Eternal justice!

SCENE VI.

Herod, Idamas, Guards.

Herod: Let me not hear her named: perfidious woman! Well, my brave soldiers, are there yet more foes?

Idamas: The Romans are subdued; the Hebrews bend Once more submissive to the yoke; and Varus, Covered with wounds, to thy victorious arm Gives up the field: O thou hast gained this day Eternal glory; but the prætor's blood, Shed by thy hand, will draw on thee the vengeance Of proud offended Rome: a crime like this—

Herod: And now for my revenge on Mariamne. Unworthy of my love I cast her from me, And from this moment shall begin to reign. O! I was blind, that fond destructive passion Was Herod's only weakness: let her die: Let me forget her charms, and her remembrance Be blotted now forever from my soul. Are all things ready for the execution?

Idamas: They are, my lord.

Herod: How quickly they obey me! Unhappy Herod! must she perish then? Didst thou say, Idamas, 'twas ready all?

Idamas: The guards have seized her person, and too soon Thy vengeance will be satisfied.

Herod: She courted Her own destruction, and obliged me to it: But she is gone: I'll think no more on it: Oh! I could have lived and died with Mariamne: To what hast thou compelled me?

SCENE the last.

Herod, Idamas, Nabal.

Herod: Nabal, ha! Whither so fast? just heaven! and in tears! How my soul shakes with dreadful apprehension.

Nabal: My lord—

Herod: What wouldst thou say?

Nabal: My feeble voice Dies on my trembling lips.

Herod: O Mariamne!

Nabal: Superfluous sorrow!

Herod: Ha! 'tis past then, is it?

Nabal: She is no more.

Herod: Ha! dead! great God!

Nabal: My lord, Permit me, 'tis a debt I owe to thee, Due to her memory, to her virtues due, To show thee what a treasure thou hast lost, The worth of that dear blood which thou hast shed: Know, Herod, she was never faithless to thee; But, even whilst Varus fought for her, refused His offered hand, slighted his ardent vows, And hazarded her life to succor thee.

Herod: What do I hear? O wretched Herod! Nabal, What has thou told me?

Nabal: In that very moment, Even when her generous heart inspired her last And noblest act, thy cruel orders came, And she was led to death: thy barbarous sister Urged on her fate.

Herod: Inhuman Salome; Why did my justice spare that cruel monster? What punishments must be reserved for thee! But let thy blood and mine—Nabal, go on, And kill me with the melancholy tale.

Nabal: How shall I speak the rest! the guard, thou knowest, By thee directed, led her hence: she followed Without a murmur or reproach of thee; Without affected pride, or real fear; On her fair front sat graceful majesty, Tempered with softness; modest innocence And heart-felt virtue sparkled in her eyes; Her sorrows gave new lustre to her charms; Priests, Hebrews, all, with tears and shrieks besought her: The soldiers called for death, and wept the fate Of Mariamne—and of Herod too; For deep, they cried aloud, would be thy grief, And horror and remorse attend thee ever.

Herod: How every word strikes to my heart!

Nabal: She felt For their distress, and as she passed along, Spake comfort to them. To the fatal scaffold At length she came; there lifted up her hands, Loaded with shameful chains, and thus she spake: "Farewell, unhappy king; Herod, farewell! Thy dying Mariamne weeps for thee, And thee alone; may this be thy last act Of foul injustice! may thy reign henceforth Be happy! Take my people to thy care; Protect my children; love and cherish them; And I shall die content." She spake, and bent Her beauteous body to the axe; I saw, And wept her fall.

Herod: Then Mariamne's dead; And Herod lives: thou dear, and honored shade! Ye poor remains of all that once was fair And good, and virtuous, to the silent grave Soon will I follow thee—Ye shall not stop me, Perfidious subjects: from my murderous hand, Why will ye wrest my sword? O Mariamne! Come now, and be avenged: tear forth this heart That bleeds for thee. I faint, I die. [He faints.]

Nabal: His senses Are lost; his grief o'erpowers him.

Herod: What thick clouds O'erspread my troubled soul! deep melancholy Weighs down my senses; why am I abandoned, Left to my sorrows thus? No sister here; No Mariamne! How you stand and weep At distance from me! Dare you not approach me! All Judah flies before her wretched king. What have I done? why am I thus abhorred? Who will relieve me? who will soothe my grief? Fetch Mariamne to me.

Nabal: Mariamne, My lord!

Herod: Ay, bring her; for I know the sight Of her will calm at once my agony: When Mariamne's with me, my blessed hours Are all serene, and life glides sweetly on: Methinks her very name hath healed my woes, And lessened my affliction: let her come.

Nabal: My lord—

Herod: I'll see her.

Nabal: Sir, have you forgot That Mariamne's dead?

Herod: What sayest thou?

Nabal: Grief Transports him; his mind's hurt; he's not himself.

Herod: Ha! Mariamne dead! destructive reason, Why comest thou now to tell me this sad truth? Down with these hateful walls, this fatal palace, Stained with her blood, and let its ruins hide The accursed place where Mariamne perished! Is she then dead, and I her murderer! Punish this parricide, this horrid monster:

Tear him in pieces, you who weep her loss, My subjects; and thou, heaven, who hast her now, Send down thy vengeful lightnings, and destroy me.

End

www.ingramcontent.com/pod-product-compliance
Lightning Source LLC
Chambersburg PA
CBHW021121020426
42331CB00004B/571